DIALLO BROOKS

Bold Quiet Warrior

Leadership as a Disciplined Practice in Service of Justice

"Service is the rent we pay for the privilege of living on this earth."

Shirley Chisholm

Contents

Acknowledgments

This book grew out of a life shaped by people, relationships, and moments that taught me far more than I could ever capture on my own.

I am deeply grateful to my mother, **Nancy Ware**, whose life and leadership shaped my earliest understanding of responsibility, restraint, and care. Long before I had language for leadership, I learned from her that authority is most meaningful when it is exercised with humility, preparation, and love. Her example continues to guide both my work and my practice.

I am also thankful for my grandparents, **St. Elmo Crawford, Sr.** and **Mamie Evelyn Crawford**, whose presence and guidance helped shape my early development. Through them, and through the wider fabric of my family, I learned the importance of grounding one's life in values, community, and a sense of responsibility that extends beyond oneself.

I am grateful for my father, **Luther Brooks**, for the life lessons he shared, even amid challenge, and for the opportunity to reconnect and know one another more fully. I am also deeply thankful for my step-father, **Robert Ware**, whose steady presence and example taught me what it means to be a responsible man—to show up with consistency, care, and accountability. Though both are no longer here, their influence remains with me.

I am thankful for my siblings—**Dalila, Omari, Elizabeth, Obataiye (Oba), and Ayinde**—for the way we have grown together, challenged one another, and stayed connected through every season. Our shared history, laughter, disagreements, and love have kept me grounded and reminded me that leadership begins at home—with relationship, accountability, and respect.

I extend my gratitude to my aunts, uncles, cousins, and extended family, whose care, perspective, and shared history have continually reinforced the importance of belonging, accountability, and staying rooted. Their influence is woven into this work in ways both seen and unseen.

I am deeply thankful for the movement leaders who have shaped me—especially grassroots organizers, young and emerging leaders, and those on the frontlines of social and racial justice work who labor every day, often without recognition, to strengthen their communities. Their energy, consistency, passion, and dedication have challenged me, taught me, and continue to shape how I understand leadership, responsibility, and what it means to stay accountable to the work.

I am also thankful for the mentors, colleagues, and partners who invested in my development as a leader—through personal interaction, steady example, and the willingness to challenge my views. Their leadership, practiced in real time and real relationship, helped expand my understanding of what effective and responsible leadership can be.

This is my first manuscript, and I owe particular gratitude to those who encouraged its development when it was still uncertain—who reminded me that reflection is not retreat, and that naming one's practice can be an act of generosity.

Finally, I thank my wife, **Carrie**, and my children, **Marvin, Najah, and Diallo**, who continually reinforce my reason for doing this work. I am especially grateful for my grandson, **Ade Brooks**, whose presence reminds me that leadership is always about the future we are preparing, whether we will see it fully or not. I am also thankful for the friends who keep me grounded and real, offering perspective, honesty, and companionship along the way. Together, they keep me clear about the kind of leadership—and the kind of world—I hope to help build.

Author's Note

Leadership didn't enter my life as a goal I set out to pursue. It grew quietly, shaped by the people who raised me, the communities that held me, and the expectations that came with being taught—early on—to pay attention, take responsibility, and care for more than just myself.

Long before I understood titles or institutions, I understood responsibility. I grew up surrounded by family—parents, grandparents, aunts, uncles, cousins, and family friends—who believed that paying attention to the world was not optional. Being a good citizen and a good human being meant understanding what was happening around you and deciding how you would respond to it. Justice was not an abstract concept. It was something you talked about, argued over, and carried with you.

Just as important as those conversations was the love that surrounded them. I was raised in a family where love showed up consistently—sometimes quietly, sometimes fiercely—but always with intention. Author bell hooks reminds us that love is an action, not a feeling. That understanding shaped how I see leadership. In my view, good leadership must be centered in love—not as softness, but as commitment. Love that holds people accountable. Love that shows up in difficult moments. Love that believes people are worth fighting for.

The phrase *Bold Quiet Warrior* comes from the meaning of my first and middle name, Diallo Kamau. Growing up in a household deeply connected to our African roots as Black people in America shaped who I became from an early age. From the African names given to my siblings and me, to the principles of Kwanzaa that guided our values, I was taught to honor heritage, community, and collective responsibility. Concepts like Umoja (unity) and Ujima (collective work and responsibility) were not slogans; they were expectations.

Over time, I came to understand that *Bold Quiet Warrior* also describes a way of moving through the world. Boldness without losing oneself to ego. Quiet without passivity. A warrior not defined by aggression, but by endurance, preparation, and the discipline required to fight for justice and liberation.

This book is not a memoir in the traditional sense. It is a reflection on leadership as a practice—one that must be learned, tested, refined, and recommitted to over time. It is shaped by my experiences organizing communities, leading national campaigns, working inside philanthropy and government, and building institutions meant to outlast any one individual. It is also shaped by something much more fundamental: the way I learned to listen, love, and respond when things were hard.

We live in a moment that rewards volume over substance and speed over thoughtfulness. Too often, leadership is confused with visibility, and impact is measured by attention rather than outcomes. *Bold Quiet Warrior* offers a different path. It argues that real change requires leaders who are willing to slow down, learn deeply, listen carefully, and sharpen their skills with intention. Leaders who understand that justice work is not about being right— it is about being responsible.

This book is an invitation—not to follow my path, but to reflect on your own. To consider how you lead, how you listen, and how you respond to both success and struggle. Because leadership is not defined only by what goes well, but by how we grow through what doesn't.

"Love is an action, never simply a feeling." — bell hooks

Introduction

Bold Quiet Warrior is an invitation to unlock the leader already in you.

Not through volume or visibility, but through practice—through preparation, responsibility, and care.

Drawing from a life shaped by family legacy, movement work, and leadership inside institutions, Diallo K. Brooks reflects on the quiet disciplines that sustain change over time. This book does not offer formulas or shortcuts. Instead, it explores what leadership asks of us when the spotlight fades: earning voice through preparation, stewarding power without ego, honoring capacity, and building what lasts.

Bold Quiet Warrior speaks to organizers, public servants, institution-build ers, and anyone who feels the pull of responsibility but resists performative leadership. It is for those who understand that leadership is not something bestowed or claimed—it is something already present, waiting to be practiced with intention.

This is not a story about arrival. It is an invitation to alignment. To lead from where you are. To stay when the work is slow.

Leadership does not always announce itself. Sometimes it begins quietly, when you choose to step forward.

Bold Quiet Warrior invites you to unlock that choice.

Chapter One — Lessons Learned at Home

Before I ever stood at a podium, before I organized a meeting or led a campaign, leadership was taught to me at my grandparents' house. That house sat in Washington, DC—a place that carried history not as abstraction but as lived experience. It was where family gathered, stories were told, and disagreements unfolded with rigor and respect. It was where I learned that voice had to be earned, not assumed. Preparation mattered. Listening came before speaking.

My grandmother, Mamie Crawford Walker, anchored our family in a lineage of institution-builders and justice advocates. Her home was not a museum, although history lived there. It was a classroom. And the lessons were not delivered through lectures but through expectation. You came prepared. You paid attention. You understood that what you said carried weight—not because of who you were related to, but because of how you showed up.

That classroom was shaped just as powerfully by my grandfather.

St. Elmo Crawford Sr., my maternal grandfather, was a strong and confident man from Jacksonville, Florida. A military veteran, a business owner, and a graduate of Howard University, he carried himself with a quiet authority that never needed explanation. He was deeply learned—extremely well-read, disciplined, and thoughtful—but also completely at ease in many different settings. I watched him move seamlessly from his dental practice to the golf course, from professional spaces to the community, never shrinking and never performing.

In his younger days, he boxed. He played basketball. He told stories about coming into his own when he first moved to Washington, DC—navigating a city that demanded toughness, awareness, and self-respect. Those stories were not told to impress. They were offered as lessons about dignity, survival, and knowing who you are in environments that test you.

As a child, I saw him as a tall, imposing figure—strong, steady, and protective. But what stayed with me just as deeply was his compassion. He was loving, attentive, and present with me and with our family. That combination—strength without cruelty, confidence without arrogance—left a lasting imprint. He taught me what it meant to be a strong Black man who did not need to announce himself to be known.

My grandparents met at Howard University, where they both graduated. My grandfather would later attend dental school, continuing a tradition of discipline, scholarship, and service. Howard was not just an institution in our family; it was a throughline. My mother, Nancy Ware, would later graduate from Howard as well. Spottswood Robinson III—my grandmother's cousin and a litigator in *Brown v. Board of Education*—was a graduate of Howard University School of Law and later served as a professor and dean. Education, in our family, was never separate from responsibility.

I grew up knowing that my great-great grandmother, Maggie Lena Walker, had built institutions when the world insisted Black people were incapable of doing so. My grandmother had grown up in Maggie Walker's house as a child, absorbing that legacy not as history, but as expectation. Her house now stands as a National Historic Site in Richmond, Virginia. Her legacy is taught in textbooks, but in our family her story was not mythology. It was responsibility.

That responsibility was reinforced by my mother, Nancy Ware, who became my first and most demanding leadership mentor. She did not shield me from the world's complexity. She invited me into it. Our conversations—sometimes gentle, sometimes sharp—were apprenticeships in real time. She taught me that leadership is not about being right, but about being prepared. Not about dominating space, but about stewarding it.

3

As a child, I often wanted to speak before I was ready. I wanted to be part of the conversation immediately. But the lesson was consistent: listen first. Learn the room. Do the work. Then speak.

That discipline stayed with me.

It shaped how I moved through school, organizing spaces, and rooms where power was present and temptation was real. It taught me that leadership was not granted by proximity or pedigree. It was earned through practice, humility, and consistency.

This early formation mattered because it grounded me long before I encountered formal leadership roles. It gave me a framework for understanding power—not as something to chase, but as something to handle carefully. It taught me that visibility was a tool, not a goal. And it instilled a belief that leadership, at its best, is quiet, prepared, and accountable.

The first classroom did not teach me how to win. It taught me how to listen and wait. It taught me how to carry history without being consumed by it and how to honor legacy without hiding behind it.

Those lessons would be tested again and again—in movement spaces, institutions, and moments of grief and pressure. But they began there, at my grandparents' house, where leadership was never abstract and never optional.

It was simply expected.

What I did not yet know was how often those early lessons would be tested—and how much they would ask of me once the work moved beyond the walls of that house.

2

Chapter Two — Encouraged Into Leadership Before I Saw It in Myself

I didn't arrive at Shepherd looking for leadership. I came to play basketball, get my degree, and stay out of the way.

What I didn't realize was that the lessons I carried with me would be tested almost immediately.

As a Black kid from Washington, DC suddenly living in rural West Virginia, I was focused on what felt safe and familiar. Basketball was familiar. Books were familiar. The small circle of Black students—mostly athletes—was familiar. Everything else felt like something to navigate, not something to join.

My first semester didn't go as planned. An injury sent me home before I ever really got started. Coming back required more than physical recovery. It meant deciding that I still belonged there, even when the place didn't always feel like it was built with me in mind. When I returned, I stayed close to my lane: practice, class, study hall, sleep. Repeat. I wasn't trying to be known. I was trying to make it.

The shift began with someone who saw something in me long before I recognized it myself.

His name was Bill—my RA, a little older than the rest of us, and one of the most spirited people on campus. He was the kind of person who showed up to games painted in school colors, yelling like he was part of the pep band. He was White, from a DC suburb, and he had a way of connecting with us without pretending to be something he wasn't. He looked out for the guys on our wing. He paid attention.

One afternoon he stopped me in the hallway and said he was running for student government. He wanted me on his ticket as President Pro Tempore. I laughed. I told him I wasn't trying to do all that. I was a political science major, sure, but that didn't mean I wanted to be in student government at Shepherd. I was still trying to get my footing academically and get back on the court.

He didn't let it go.

He told me I had a steadiness about me. That I asked questions other people didn't ask. That I carried myself with a seriousness that student government needed. He said being from DC—Chocolate City, a place where Black leadership wasn't an exception—gave me a perspective the campus didn't have enough of. He said the conversations we had in the hallway, the way I thought about fairness and systems, the way I listened before I spoke... all of that belonged in the rooms where decisions were being made.

I didn't see it as leadership. I saw it as surviving with my eyes open.

But he kept pushing, and eventually I said yes.

That yes changed the trajectory of my time at Shepherd.

Winning that election put me in rooms I never expected to be in. Suddenly I was sitting across from administrators, hearing how decisions were made, watching who spoke first and who never spoke at all. I saw how student life was shaped, who had influence, and—more importantly—who didn't. I realized quickly that if I didn't speak up, the experiences of Black students, especially Black athletes, would never be part of the equation.

I wasn't trying to be a spokesperson. I was trying to be honest about what I saw and lived.

I talked about what it felt like to be one of the few Black students in a classroom. I talked about the assumptions people made about us before we opened our mouths. I talked about the difference between being visible and being valued. And I learned that when you speak from lived experience—not performance, not anger, not ego—people listen differently. They may not always agree, but they hear you.

Growing up in DC shaped that confidence. I had seen Black leadership my whole life—mayors, teachers, coaches, community elders. I didn't walk into rooms assuming I had to shrink. I walked in knowing I had something to contribute.

Student government became the first place I practiced leadership out loud.

It taught me that leadership often begins with someone else's belief in you. It taught me that sometimes the door opens before you feel ready to walk through it. It taught me that leadership isn't always about wanting the role— it's about recognizing the responsibility once you're in it.

Bill saw something in me that I hadn't yet named. His encouragement didn't just change my involvement on campus; it changed my understanding of myself. It was the first time I stepped into leadership not because I was chasing it, but because someone I trusted said, "You belong here."

That mattered. It still does.

3

Chapter Three — Learning to Earn Voice

I learned early that wanting to speak was not the same as being ready to be heard.

As a young person, I was eager, curious, and opinionated. I wanted to be part of important conversations about justice, leadership, and what needed to change, but eagerness alone did not grant access. In the spaces that shaped me, voice was not something to be claimed. It was something to be earned.

That understanding followed me to Shepherd University, where opportunity arrived before readiness.

College became my first real testing ground outside the family circle. It was where theory met practice, where ideals collided with institutional reality, and where leadership stopped being abstract. I arrived with conviction, but conviction without discipline quickly revealed its limits. Being elected didn't make me ready; it made me accountable.

I found my footing through organizing.

United Brothers became a formative space for me—not because it offered a title but because it demanded responsibility. Building that organization required listening to peers whose experiences differed from my own. It required navigating skepticism, resistance, and the slow work of trust-building. It required learning how to move ideas from conversation into structure.

This was also where mentorship deepened.

Rev. Ernest Lyles Sr., director of the Multicultural Leadership Program, did not flatter ambition. He sharpened it. Through retreats, reflection, and rigorous dialogue, he taught me that leadership was not about volume or charisma; it was about clarity and consistency. He pushed me to interrogate my motivations and to understand that leadership development was not a sprint but a long apprenticeship.

Athletics reinforced these lessons in a different register.

Basketball demanded discipline, preparation, and accountability to a team. I could not shortcut my effort. I could not hide from my weaknesses. I learned quickly that leadership meant showing up when tired, staying focused under pressure, and trusting others to do their part. The court became another classroom—one where ego was exposed and teamwork was non-negotiable.

Across these spaces, a pattern emerged.

Voice followed work.

The more I listened, the more I learned. The more I prepared, the more confidence followed. The more I centered collective success over personal recognition, the more influence I gained. Leadership was not something I stepped into all at once; it unfolded gradually, shaped by feedback, failure, and growth.

There were moments when I stumbled. I sometimes spoke too soon or underestimated the complexity of the work. Those moments were instructive. They taught me that leadership required humility—not as posture but as practice.

By the time I left Shepherd, I carried more than credentials. I carried a framework. Leadership was not about being the loudest voice in the room. It was about being the most prepared, the most accountable, and the most willing to learn.

Earning a voice meant earning trust.

That understanding guided me into movement spaces beyond campus— where the stakes were higher, the work was more urgent, and the lessons were even sharper.

4

Chapter Four — Reengagement and Discernment

B y the time I reached my sophomore year at Shepherd, I had begun to understand that leadership required discipline, preparation, and earning trust. But knowing that didn't mean I always felt grounded. Even as I stayed committed to basketball, I was quietly wrestling with whether it was something I wanted to continue. My love for the game was still there, yet my sense of belonging felt unsettled. I was navigating a campus and community that often felt unfamiliar, and I began to wonder if I might thrive more fully in a different, more welcoming environment.

That questioning did not happen in isolation.

Family and friends noticed the tension I was carrying and began asking me honest, grounding questions: *What do you want? What kind of environment do you need to grow?* The conversations weren't about pressure or persuasion. They were about permission—permission to consider transferring, permission to imagine something different, and permission to be honest about what I was experiencing.

Those moments mattered.

They reminded me that leadership is not always about certainty. Sometimes it begins in discernment. In allowing yourself to name discomfort without rushing to escape it. And in recognizing that being seen does not always mean being told what to do—it means being trusted to decide.

Staying at Shepherd was not the obvious choice.

It meant committing to a place that still challenged me. It meant choosing to build rather than leave. Leadership, in that moment, looked like accountability to myself. It meant showing up fully, even when the environment required more effort to navigate. It meant investing in relationships, culture, and purpose where I was, rather than assuming growth only existed somewhere else.

That season reshaped how I understood encouragement.

Encouragement was not reassurance. It was a challenge. It was people believing enough in me to trust my capacity to choose with integrity. It was leadership expressed through care, patience, and honest reflection.

That experience sharpened my understanding of capacity.

I learned that questioning does not mean quitting. Sometimes it means recalibrating. Sometimes it means deciding to stay and build rather than start over. Leadership demanded that I be honest about where I was and intentional about what I was willing to commit to.

This chapter of my journey reinforced a lesson that would follow me into every leadership space that came after: people do not always need to be pushed forward. Sometimes they need to be seen clearly. Given space to decide. Trusted to grow where they stand.

Leadership, at its best, recognizes when to offer each.

5

Chapter Five — Entering the Work

L eadership becomes real when the work leaves the classroom. After Shepherd, the questions that had once been theoretical became immediate. Justice was no longer something to debate; it was something to organize for, with real consequences. The work moved from campus rooms into communities carrying urgency, accountability, and high stakes.

My early movement work was not glamorous.

It was long days and late nights. It was knocking on doors, facilitating meetings, and listening more than speaking. It was learning how to build trust with people who had every reason to be skeptical. It was understanding that leadership in these spaces was not about being impressive; it was about being reliable.

I entered organizing with humility.

I did not arrive as an expert. I arrived as a learner. Communities had already been doing the work long before I showed up. My role was to support, amplify, and help connect efforts across geography and issue areas. Leadership meant honoring local wisdom and resisting the urge to impose solutions from the outside.

This period taught me the discipline of listening. Listening to returning citizens navigating reentry. Listening to young people demanding a future that felt increasingly uncertain. Listening to elders who had seen cycles of attention come and go. Each conversation carried lessons about resilience, frustration, and hope grounded in realism rather than rhetoric.

Movement work also introduced me to coalition-building.

Coalitions are fragile by nature. They bring together organizations with different histories, priorities, and power dynamics. Leadership in these spaces required patience. It required clarity about shared goals and honesty about differences. It required the ability to hold tension without forcing false consensus.

I learned quickly that urgency can be both a motivator and a liability.

The pressure to act—to respond to injustice in real time—was constant, but speed without strategy often led to burnout or fragmentation. Leadership demanded that I balance urgency with sustainability and think not just about the next action, but about the long arc of the work.

This chapter of my journey grounded me in the realities of movement-building.

It taught me that leadership is not about being at the center; it is about strengthening the edges. It is about creating pathways for others to lead. It is about staying accountable to the people most impacted by the work, even when that accountability is uncomfortable.

Entering the work clarified something essential: leadership is not an abstract calling. It is a daily practice, shaped by discipline, humility, and a willingness to stay when the work is hard and the outcomes are uncertain.

Those lessons followed me into national spaces, where the scale would change but the fundamentals would not.

6

Chapter Six — Carrying Legacy Without Inheriting Ego

"I am not satisfied with simply knowing. I must apply. I am not satisfied with simply believing. I must act." — Maggie Lena Walker

Legacy has a way of introducing itself before you are ready.

Long before I fully understood the weight of my family's history, I felt its presence. It showed up in questions people asked, expectations they carried, and assumptions—both generous and limiting—about who I was and what I should become. Being connected to a lineage of institution-builders and justice advocates meant that history often entered the room before I did.

That reality forced an early reckoning.

I knew the names. Maggie Lena Walker. Spottswood Robinson. I knew the stories—a family rooted in building when exclusion was the rule, not the exception. But what mattered most inside our home was not recognition; it was responsibility. Legacy was never framed as entitlement. It was framed as obligation.

My mother was clear about this. She did not allow me to borrow credibility from history. She insisted that I earn my own. Her mentorship was not about shielding me from pressure; it was about preparing me to carry it without arrogance. She reminded me often that legacy could open doors, but it could not keep them open. Only discipline, humility, and integrity could do that.

There were moments when I struggled with this balance—when I felt the pull to live up to something larger than myself, when I worried about falling short, when I questioned whether my work would ever feel sufficient in the shadow of those who came before me. Those tensions were real, and they shaped how I approached leadership.

What I learned over time is that legacy is not something you perform; it is something you steward.

Stewardship means resisting the temptation to lead from name recognition rather than relationship. It means grounding work in service rather than symbolism. It means understanding that honoring history requires building something meaningful in the present, not simply referencing the past.

Stewarding legacy became especially important as my work expanded into national spaces. As visibility increased, so did the risk of ego. Titles, platforms, and proximity to power can distort purpose if you are not careful. Legacy, when misunderstood, can become a shield—something used to deflect critique or justify missteps.

I refused that path.

Instead, I committed to letting my work speak for itself. I committed to being accountable to the people I served, not the stories attached to my name, and to remembering that leadership is practiced, not inherited.

Carrying legacy without inheriting ego required constant self-reflection. It demanded that I stay teachable, remain open to correction, and continue to learn from those whose experiences differed from my own. It reminded me that leadership rooted in humility is more durable than leadership rooted in reputation.

This chapter of my journey clarified something essential: history is not a pedestal; it is a foundation. And foundations are meant to support growth, not replace it.

As I moved forward into larger movements and more complex institutions, this understanding anchored me. It kept me grounded when recognition came. It steadied me when criticism followed. And it reinforced a truth I carry with me still: legacy is about being responsible, not about being remembered.

7

Chapter Seven — Leadership Under Pressure

"Everybody can be great because everybody can serve." — Martin Luther King Jr.

Pressure has a way of clarifying who you are.

By the time I stepped into national campaigns and coalition leadership, the stakes had changed. The rooms were bigger. The timelines were tighter. The consequences of missteps were more visible. Decisions moved faster, and the margin for error felt thinner. Leadership was no longer just about building trust; it was about sustaining it under scrutiny.

National work introduced a different rhythm.

Campaigns demanded urgency without sacrificing strategy. Coalitions required alignment across organizations with distinct histories, priorities, and power dynamics. Everyone arrived with their own expectations, constituencies, and sense of what was at risk. Leadership in these spaces required steadiness and the ability to absorb tension without transmitting it.

I learned quickly that pressure does not create character; it reveals it.

In moments of stress, habits surfaced. Some leaders became rigid. Others became reactive. Some retreated into control. Others avoided decision-making altogether. I had to confront my own tendencies—where I rushed, where I hesitated, and where fear of getting it wrong threatened to override clarity.

Coalition leadership tested my commitment to shared power.

It was tempting at times to move unilaterally, to push forward when consensus felt slow or fragile. But I had learned enough by then to know that speed without alignment often creates more work later. Leadership under pressure demanded patience, even when urgency screamed otherwise.

I also saw how power shifted behavior.

Proximity to influence can distort priorities. Fear—of losing access, funding, or relevance—can lead people to compromise values quietly. At times I was forced to define my boundaries and decide what I was willing to trade and what I was not. Leadership requires discernment, not just ambition.

There were wins—moments when collective effort moved policy, shifted narrative, or expanded participation. And there were losses—campaigns that fell short, strategies that didn't land, and relationships strained by stress and expectation. Each outcome carried lessons. None were wasted.

What sustained me through this period was grounding.

I returned to the principles formed earlier—listening, preparation, and humility—and remembered that leadership was not about being the hero of the story, but about stewarding the work responsibly. Pressure demanded integrity more than charisma.

This chapter also revealed the importance of care.

Burnout was not theoretical; it was present, visible, and costly. I learned that leadership required pacing, not just endurance. Rest was not retreat; it was strategy. Caring for teams was not a distraction from the work; it was essential to sustaining it.

Leadership under pressure is not about perfection.

It is about integrity. About making choices you can stand by when the moment passes and the noise fades. About staying aligned when the stakes are high and the path is unclear.

These lessons followed me into institutions, where pressure took on new forms and the work of stewardship became even more complex.

8

Chapter Eight — Stewardship Inside Institutions

Movement work teaches you how to build power. Institutions teach you how power moves.

When I stepped into philanthropic and institutional spaces, the terrain shifted again. The urgency of organizing was still present, but it was filtered through process, governance, and long-term strategy. Decisions were no longer just about what should happen; they were about what could happen within systems designed to manage risk.

This chapter is about stewardship.

Inside institutions, leadership is less visible but no less consequential. Resources move quietly. Decisions ripple outward over time. The work is often misunderstood from the outside, dismissed as slow or compromised. But I came to understand that institutions, when stewarded with intention, can be powerful tools for change.

Stewardship required a different posture.

I was no longer just advocating for ideas; I was responsible for moving resources, shaping strategy, and supporting organizations doing frontline work. That responsibility demanded care. It required understanding the weight of decisions that affected livelihoods, programs, and communities far beyond the room.

I learned quickly that access changes expectations.

Being inside meant seeing constraints more clearly—legal frameworks, fiduciary responsibility, and political realities. Leadership here was not about abandoning values; it was about translating them into structures that could endure scrutiny and scale. It required patience, precision, and a willingness to engage complexity without losing purpose.

This work sharpened my understanding of power dynamics.

Philanthropy sits at an intersection of influence and accountability. Without discipline, it can reinforce inequity rather than disrupt it. Stewardship demanded that I ask hard questions: Who decides? Who benefits? Who is missing from the table? Leadership meant pushing institutions to align their practices with their stated values—not through confrontation alone, but through persistent engagement.

I also learned the importance of humility.

Institutions carry history—both good and harmful. Entering these spaces required respect for institutional memory and an honest reckoning with past failures. Leadership meant listening to those who had been holding the work long before I arrived and recognizing that change often comes through accumulation rather than rupture.

This chapter reinforced a truth that guided me forward: stewardship is not passive.

It is an active responsibility—the discipline of holding power carefully, moving resources with intention, and remembering that leadership inside institutions is about care more than control.

As my work continued to expand, this understanding prepared me for the next shift—where stewardship met government, and leadership required navigating systems at scale.

9

Chapter Nine — The Pivot

The reckoning didn't arrive as a crisis. It arrived as a quiet accumulation—a weight I had been carrying for years without naming. I had been moving fast, saying yes out of obligation, showing up out of instinct, and leading from a place that looked strong on the outside but was slowly hollowing me out on the inside. I told myself I was doing what leaders do: pushing through, holding it together, staying in motion.

But motion is not the same as meaning.

And pace is not the same as purpose.

What finally caught up with me wasn't exhaustion alone. It was the realization that I had been leading from depletion, not discipline. I had been offering guidance without giving myself space to listen. I had been pouring into others while quietly running dry. And the people closest to me—the ones who loved me without condition—could see it long before I could.

This chapter marks the moment when I had to confront the gap between the leader I believed myself to be and the leader I was becoming. It was a moment of truth that asked me to slow down long enough to see myself clearly—not the version shaped by expectations, titles, or the demands of the work, but the version shaped by my values, my family's legacy, and the quiet wisdom I had been too busy to hear.

The reckoning wasn't dramatic. It was honest.

It wasn't about failure. It was about clarity.

I began to understand that leadership rooted in urgency is fragile. It burns bright but burns out. Leadership rooted in reflection, however, is durable. It can hold complexity, withstand pressure, and grow.

I had to unlearn the habits I inherited from systems that reward exhaustion and confuse sacrifice with effectiveness. I had to release the belief that being everywhere meant I was needed, or that carrying everything meant I was strong. I had to reclaim a quieter, more grounded way of leading—one that honored my humanity as much as my responsibility.

In that season, I learned:

Silence is not absence. It is preparation.

Slowing down is not retreat. It is stewardship.

Leadership is not measured by how much you carry, but by how intentionally you move.

This reckoning reshaped my understanding of responsibility. It taught me that the work is not to prove myself, but to prepare myself. Not to be the loudest voice, but the most present one. Not to lead from performance, but from practice.

This was the moment I stopped performing leadership and began living it.

It was the pivot point—the shift from urgency to intention, from over-functioning to alignment, and from inherited patterns to chosen ones.

Everything that follows in this book grows out of this pivot.

This is where the quiet became powerful.

10

Chapter Ten — Capacity, Grief, and the Cost of Carrying

Leadership carries weight long before it shows results.

By the time I reached this phase of my journey, I had accumulated experience, access, and responsibility. I had learned how to move through systems, steward power, and translate values across spaces. What I had not fully reckoned with was the cost of carrying all of it at once.

This chapter is about capacity.

Capacity is not just about skill or stamina. It is about emotional bandwidth, grief, and the unseen labor of holding responsibility while navigating loss, uncertainty, and expectation. Leadership does not pause for personal hardship, but the body and spirit keep score.

Grief entered my life not as a single event, but as a series of reckonings.

Losses layered on top of one another—personal, familial, communal. Each one demanded attention, even as the work continued. I learned quickly that grief does not announce itself politely. It shows up in fatigue, distraction, and moments when clarity feels just out of reach.

For a long time, I tried to outwork it.

I told myself that staying busy showed resilience and that pushing through was strength. I believed leadership required endurance above all else. But there is a difference between endurance and erosion, and I was learning that distinction the hard way.

This period forced me to confront my limits—not as failure, but as fact. I could not carry everything. I could not be everything to everyone. Leadership demanded honesty—not just with others, but with myself. I had to learn how to name when my capacity was stretched thin and to ask for support without shame.

This was not easy.

Movement culture often rewards sacrifice without interrogating sustainability. Institutions often expect output without accounting for humanity. Navigating both required a re-calibration of what leadership meant in practice. Care was no longer optional; it was essential.

I began to understand that tending to grief was not a detour from the work. It was part of it.

Grief clarified priorities. It stripped away performative urgency and revealed what truly mattered. It reminded me that leadership is not about constant motion; it is about presence—showing up fully, even when that means slowing down.

This chapter reshaped my relationship to rest.

Rest was not retreat. It was repair. It was an act of stewardship—of self, relationships, and the work itself. Leadership that ignores capacity eventually collapses under its own weight. Leadership that honors it becomes more durable.

Carrying responsibility over time requires discernment.

Knowing when to push. Knowing when to pause. Knowing when to ask for help. These are not signs of weakness; they are markers of maturity. Leadership, I learned, is not proven by how much you can endure, but by how wisely you choose what to carry.

This understanding informed every chapter that followed, especially as the work moved deeper into systems, reflection, and the long arc of change.

11

Chapter Eleven — Embedded, Not Absorbed

G overnment does not move at the speed of movement. That truth became unavoidable when I stepped into federal service as a Senior Equity Fellow at the U.S. Department of Education. The work was no longer about pushing from the outside; it was about translating values from within. Translation, I learned, is its own form of leadership.

Inside government, everything is layered. Authority is distributed. Decision-making is procedural. Progress is often incremental, shaped by regulation, statute, and political reality. The urgency I carried from movement spaces did not disappear, but it had to be re-calibrated.

Being embedded inside a federal agency required discipline.

I had to learn how to navigate bureaucracy without becoming absorbed by it. I learned to move ideas through systems designed to minimize risk and to advocate for equity in spaces where language was cautious and timelines were long. Leadership here was not about disruption; it was about alignment.

What surprised me most was the depth of commitment among public servants.

Contrary to popular narratives, many of the people I worked alongside were deeply invested in doing right by students, families, and communities. They carried institutional memory and understood constraints, and they often operated with far less recognition than their work deserved. Leadership in this context required respect—for process, expertise, and the people who had been holding the work long before I arrived.

My role became one of translation.

Translating movement values into policy language. Translating community needs into actionable frameworks. Translating urgency into strategy that could survive review, revision, and implementation. This work demanded patience and precision. It required me to listen carefully, speak deliberately, and choose battles wisely.

There were moments of frustration—when progress felt slow, compromise felt uncomfortable, and the distance between intention and impact seemed wide. In those moments, I returned to a guiding principle: be embedded, not absorbed.

Being embedded meant engaging fully—learning the system, building relationships, and contributing meaningfully. Not being absorbed meant holding onto purpose, remembering why I was there, and maintaining accountability to communities beyond the walls of the institution.

This balance was not always easy, but it was necessary.

Leadership inside government is often invisible. Policy language shifts quietly. Programs reach more people because of decisions made months earlier. Systems function a little more equitably because someone insisted on asking a different question.

This chapter of my journey reinforced a truth I carry forward: change does not only happen through confrontation. It also happens through translation, patience, and disciplined engagement with systems that shape lives at scale.

Being embedded without being absorbed allowed me to contribute without losing myself.

And it prepared me for the next phase—where reflection, alignment, and honest storytelling about impact became essential.

12

Chapter Twelve — The Work Within the Work

Not all leadership is visible. Some of the most important work happens beneath the surface—inside systems, teams, and ourselves.

By the time I reached this phase of my journey, I had learned that impact is not always loud. It does not always announce itself. Often, it shows up in alignment—in moments when people who rarely agree begin to move in the same direction, or in systems that function a little more justly because someone insisted on asking a different question.

This chapter is about honoring that kind of work.

Inside institutions—especially government and large organizations— progress is rarely the result of a single decision. It is the accumulation of conversations, revisions, compromises, and persistence. It is shaped by people who show up every day, often without recognition, carrying responsibility with care.

I came to deeply respect public servants during this time.

The best of these public servants understood the constraints of the system and still worked to expand what was possible within them. They carried institutional memory and navigated complexity with integrity. Leadership here required humility—recognizing that change was not something I brought with me, but something I joined.

The work within the work also demanded honesty.

It required assessing impact without exaggeration, naming what worked and what did not, and resisting the temptation to tell a cleaner story than reality allowed. Leadership meant being accountable not just for outcomes, but for truth.

This honesty extended inward.

I had to examine my own motivations. I asked myself whether I was seeking affirmation or alignment, prioritizing visibility or sustainability, and listening as much as I was speaking. These questions were not always comfortable, but they were necessary.

The work within the work is about coherence.

It is about ensuring that values are reflected not just in mission statements, but in daily practice. Coherence shows up in how teams are supported, decisions are made, and success is defined. Leadership at this level is less about direction and more about cultivation—creating conditions where good work can take root and endure.

This chapter reminded me that leadership is not a performance. It is a practice—one that requires patience, reflection, and a willingness to be shaped by the work itself.

As I prepared to transition from this phase, I carried these lessons with me. They informed my approach to what came next, where the work returned closer to the ground and leadership was once again tested by proximity to community.

13

Chapter Thirteen — When the Work Returns to the Ground

"Not everything that is faced can be changed, but nothing can be changed until it is faced." — James Baldwin

Leadership has a way of circling back.

After years of operating at national scale—inside institutions, coalitions, and government—the work returned me closer to the ground, not as a retreat but as a re calibration. The questions were familiar, but the perspective had changed. What does leadership look like when access narrows? When visibility fades? When the work is no longer buffered by titles or infrastructure?

This chapter is about that return.

Coming back into closer proximity with community reminded me that leadership is not linear. It moves in cycles. Periods of expansion are often followed by moments of contraction—not as failure, but as necessary grounding. The work on the ground demanded the same fundamentals I had learned early on: listening, trust, consistency, and care.

What had changed was my understanding of scale.

I could see more clearly how national decisions landed locally. Policy translated—or failed to translate—into lived experience. Communities carried the consequences of systems long after attention moved elsewhere. This proximity sharpened my sense of responsibility. It reinforced the importance of staying connected to the people most impacted by the work, regardless of where leadership takes me.

Returning to the ground also required humility.

I was no longer arriving as the new voice or the fresh perspective. I was joining ongoing efforts led by people who had been holding the work through cycles of attention and neglect. Leadership here meant supporting rather than directing, contributing without dominating, and recognizing when to step forward and when to step aside.

This phase reminded me that community leadership is often quiet and sustained.

It does not wait for permission. It adapts and endures. It carries wisdom that cannot be replicated at a distance. The most durable change I witnessed during this time was not driven by headlines or funding cycles; it was driven by relationships built over years.

The work returning to the ground also clarified something essential: access is temporary, but relationships are lasting.

Titles change. Roles shift. Trust, once earned, becomes a bridge across transitions. Leadership that honors those relationships remains relevant even as context evolves.

This chapter reaffirmed my commitment to staying rooted—to ensuring that wherever my work takes me, it remains accountable to community. To remembering that leadership is not about where you stand, but about who you stand with.

As the journey continued, this grounding prepared me for the next phase— where readiness, infrastructure, and preparation for future openings became central.

14

Chapter Fourteen — Preparing for the Next Opening

L eadership is not only about responding to moments; it is about preparing for them.

By this stage of my journey, I had learned that opportunities rarely arrive fully formed. They open briefly, often unexpectedly, and close just as quickly. The difference between readiness and regret is preparation grounded in clarity, discipline, and infrastructure.

This chapter is about readiness.

After cycles of movement work, institutional leadership, and government service, I became more intentional about what it meant to be prepared—not just personally, but collectively. Preparation meant building systems that could absorb opportunity without collapsing under it. It meant developing leaders who could step in without waiting for permission. It meant ensuring that when doors opened, we were not scrambling to define purpose.

Readiness requires patience.

There were moments when it would have been easy to chase visibility or position myself prematurely. But I had learned enough to know that leadership without alignment creates fragility. Preparation demanded restraint—the willingness to wait until values, capacity, and timing converged.

This phase of my work focused on infrastructure.

On strengthening organizations. On mentoring leaders. On clarifying strategy. It was less about immediate wins and more about long-term positioning. Leadership here was quiet, deliberate, and often unseen.

I also learned that readiness is relational.

No opening is navigated alone. The strength of your relationships determines how effectively you can move when the moment arrives. Trust built over time becomes currency in moments of transition. Leadership means investing in those relationships even when there is no immediate return.

Preparing for the next opening also required honesty about limits.

Not every opportunity is meant to be pursued. Discernment became as important as ambition. Leadership demanded the ability to say no—to protect capacity, honor commitments, and remain aligned with purpose.

This chapter reinforced a truth I carry forward: readiness is not passive.

It is active preparation rooted in discipline and care. It is the work you do before anyone is watching—the systems you build before they are tested and the leaders you develop before they are needed.

When the next opening comes—and it always does—preparation determines whether leadership can move with integrity and impact.

15

Chapter Fifteen — Beyond Reaction: Building What Lasts

C risis has a way of commanding attention.
In moments of urgency—after elections, during protests, or in the wake of policy shifts—leadership often becomes reactive. Energy surges. Statements are issued. Coalitions form quickly. While this response can be necessary, it is rarely sufficient. Reaction alone does not build power or create durability, and it does not sustain change.

This chapter is about moving beyond reaction.

By this point in my journey, I had seen the cycle repeat itself too many times. Moments of crisis generated momentum, only for that momentum to dissipate once attention shifted. The work surged and stalled repeatedly, never fully breaking free from the gravitational pull of urgency.

What was missing was construction.

Building what lasts requires a different posture. It demands long-term thinking in a culture that rewards immediacy. It requires investment in infrastructure rather than optics. It asks leaders to resist the temptation to chase every moment and instead commit to shaping the conditions that make progress possible over time.

This kind of leadership is quieter.

It develops leaders before they are needed, strengthens organizations during periods of relative calm, and builds coalitions prepared to act not just in response to crisis, but in pursuit of vision. It is less about reacting to what is happening and more about constructing what should exist.

I learned that durability comes from alignment.

When values, strategy, and structure are aligned, movements can withstand pressure. When they are not, even the most passionate efforts fracture under strain. Leadership required me to focus on coherence—ensuring that what we said, what we did, and how we did it reinforced one another.

This work also required patience.

Building what lasts is slow. It rarely offers immediate validation. It often unfolds outside the spotlight. This work is what makes future moments of opportunity meaningful. Without it, openings close as quickly as they appear.

Beyond reaction, leadership becomes about stewardship once again—about caring for the work in ways that outlast individual leaders and singular moments. About building institutions, relationships, and practices that can carry the work forward even when attention fades.

This chapter reaffirmed a conviction that has guided me throughout this journey: leadership is not about responding to every moment, but about preparing for the ones that matter most.

That preparation is what makes lasting change possible.

16

Chapter Sixteen — The Invitation

"I f my mind can conceive it, and my heart can believe it, then I can achieve it." — Jesse Jackson Sr.

This book was never meant to be a conclusion.

It is a pause. A moment to take stock. A chance to reflect on what leadership has demanded, what it has revealed, and what it continues to ask of us. The journey traced here is not exceptional because of titles or proximity to power. It matters because it is unfinished—and because it belongs to more than one person.

Leadership, as I have come to understand it, is not an identity. It is a practice—one that evolves with context, deepens through failure, and matures through responsibility. It is shaped by who we listen to, what we protect, and how we choose to show up when the work becomes difficult or unclear.

Throughout these chapters, a few truths have remained constant: leadership is earned, not claimed. Visibility is a tool, not a goal. Power must be stewarded, not hoarded. Care is not a detour from the work; it is part of it.

Perhaps most importantly, leadership is collective.

No one carries this work alone. Every chapter of my journey has been shaped by mentors, peers, elders, young people, and communities who taught me— sometimes gently, sometimes firmly—what it means to lead with integrity. Their influence lives in these pages, even when their names do not.

This final chapter is not meant to be a summary. It is an invitation.

An invitation to lead where you are. To prepare before the moment arrives. To listen before you speak. To build what lasts rather than chase what shines. To honor your capacity without abandoning your responsibility. And to remember that leadership is not about being the boldest voice in the room, but about being a steady presence in the work.

The world does not need more performative leadership. It needs disciplined leadership—leadership rooted in humility, clarity, and care. Leadership willing to stay when the work is slow and the outcomes uncertain. Leadership that understands that justice is not a destination, but a practice.

If this book offers anything, let it be permission to lead imperfectly, learn continuously, and use whatever access you have in service of something larger than yourself.

The work continues. The invitation stands.

And leadership—quiet, bold, and disciplined—remains a practice we choose every day.

17

A Closing Reflection: Leadership, Practiced

A Closing Reflection: Leadership, Practiced

L eadership is not an identity to claim. It is a practice we must return to.

What follows is not meant as a summary or a set of instructions. It is a collection of practical truths shaped by years of experience—offered as reference, not rule.

These truths were not learned all at once. They were shaped over time, tested in real settings, and refined through responsibility.

Leadership Is a Practice

Leadership is not who you are. It is what you do—consistently, imperfectly, and always in relationship with others.

Voice Is Earned

Preparation precedes influence. Listening comes before speaking. Trust grows through work, not position.

Visibility Is a Tool

Being seen is not the same as being effective. Visibility should serve the work, not replace it.

Boldness Does Not Require Ego

Conviction does not need dominance. Strength does not require volume. Quiet is not absence—it is often intention.

Legacy Is Stewardship

History may open doors. Responsibility keeps them open. Legacy is built through present-day choices.

Urgency Requires Discipline

Speed can mobilize. Discipline sustains. Leadership requires knowing when to move—and when to slow down.

Power Must Be Handled Carefully

Access changes behavior. Leadership demands reflection, restraint, and accountability, especially when no one is watching.

Institutions Can Be Shaped

Change does not only happen outside systems. With care and intention, institutions can become tools for justice.

Embedded Does Not Mean Absorbed

You can work within systems without losing purpose. Translation is leadership. Alignment takes effort.

Capacity Is Not Infinite

Leadership does not exempt you from limits. Honoring capacity is responsibility, not weakness.

Care Sustains the Work

Care is not a distraction. It is infrastructure.

Pressure Reveals Leadership

Stress does not create character. It exposes it. Integrity is measured in difficult moments.

Staying Matters

Leadership is not only about starting or winning. It is about staying— accountable, teachable, and present.

There Is No Final Arrival

Leadership in service of justice is ongoing. The work continues. So does the responsibility.

The Invitation

Return to the practice. Listen carefully. Prepare deeply. Act with care. Leadership remains a choice we make—again and again.

18

Standing on Shoulders

T his work did not begin with me, and it does not end here.

What I carry forward has been shaped by those who came before me—family, elders, organizers, and leaders who stepped into uncertainty with discipline and care. Their leadership was not loud or self-congratulatory. It was grounded in responsibility, collective effort, and a willingness to build what did not yet exist.

Maggie Lena Walker understood that leadership meant acting together, insisting, *"Let us put our money together; let us use our money; let us put our brains together and see what we can do for ourselves and our race."* Her words remind us that liberation has always required shared commitment and institution-building rooted in trust.

Spottswood Robinson carried that same ethic into the courts, naming plainly that *"segregation is per se inequality,"* and demanding that systems be held accountable to justice rather than comfort. His leadership was not performative, but it was unyielding—anchored in preparation, clarity, and moral resolve.

These examples come not only from my family, but from our shared history as a country. They remind us that equity has never arrived on its own. It has always required leaders willing to use their voice in service of collective liberation, to challenge what is unjust, and to stay present long after the moment passes.

This book is an invitation to that tradition.

To build the quiet warrior within. To lead with discipline rather than ego. To carry responsibility with care and grace. And to work toward a more just world—not through spectacle, but through sustained practice.

The work continues. So does the responsibility.

I am the Bold Quiet Warrior.